CW01496110

CEPHALOPRESS
www.cephalopress.com

i

Published in the UK by Cephalopress Ltd 2022

Borders & Belonging
The Cephalopress Anthology

www.cephalopress.com
info@cephalopress.com

All rights reserved
Copyright © Cephalopress Limited

This is a work of fiction. Names, characters, business-es, places, events, and incidents are either the products of the authors' imagination or used in a fictitious man-ner. Any resemblance to actual persons, living or dead, or actual events is purely coincidental.

No part of this publication may be reproduced, stored in a retrieval system, stored in a database, and/or published in any form or by any means, electronic, mechanical, photocopying, recording, or otherwise, without the prior written permission of the publisher.

ISBN   978-1-8382206-4-8

Cover design by: Diletta Arzani and Daniel Lambert

Book design by: Maté Jarai

Borders & Belonging

The Cephalopress Anthology

Contents

For those yet to find a place to call home

x

Introduction
By Christina Wilkins

Groups. Circles. Communities. Nations.

We live in an age where who we are is defined by where we belong; what spaces we inhabit, both physically and virtually, shape how others see us.

The groups we are a part of can be small, tight-knit, and offer a source of comfort. Our circles are wider, but there is often a familiarity there that keeps us a part of them.

Communities can give a huge sense of belonging. We may feel like we've found our home in them, whether that's intellectually, emotionally, or spiritually. These communities are so often held together by a virtual presence that allows for a global reach.

It is joyful to be part of, for example, a global LGBT+ community: we may recognise that our experiences are not monolithic, but the support the community has to offer is key.

Communities become big enough to speak louder, to make change happen.

This is why finding a space where we belong is so essential, especially now, in a moment where there are so many voices, that ours might feel insignificant. Belonging gives us the power of multiple, the courage and the support to speak up. Belonging can help us understand who we are.

Of course, where we belong is within spaces or communities that have borders between inner and outer. Those borders, and where we stand in relation to them, tell us whether we are accepted or not. Failure to cross a border can mean standing out in the cold, lacking a safe space where we are accepted. Borders, though they may show the limits of a group, community, or, most commonly, of nations, are electric with meaning.

Media tells us of the need to protect borders. Borders can be threatened. Insecure borders lead to the invasion of a community. But what often isn't spoken of is that this policing of borders forgets the human cost; those who belong nowhere, or who are seeking communities away from danger, or persecution.

As the anthology opens, we start with Samantha Carr's 'How to Talk to Shy People at Parties'. Carr's poem considers how 'You then won't remember the shy people are there / because in many ways they aren't'.

We begin by standing on the outskirts of the most common, and smallert of spaces in which we may feel exclusion, a lack of belonging; the party, representing the everyday social situation.
And as we move through the collection, we expand outwards. Our circles grow wider.

We begin to think about the places that define our sense of be-

2

longing: neighbourhoods, towns. The tree at the centre of Devjani Bodepudi's story 'Charlie's Tree' stands 'between us and among us', creating a focal point for the community of the cul-de-sac. The places we live can offer a rich sense of community, but some of us are not lucky enough to feel that. Even in darker moments, the connections with the neighbour we pass and know only well enough to say hello can anchor us in space and time. We become part of an ecosystem.

As the collection moves on, we see belonging to different cultures, communities and spaces, and how that belonging is enacted. It may involve a return ('Brighella'), a mapping ('How to Heal A Broken Heart') or a retelling ('Where is Home For You').

These pieces locate belonging in memories, in locations, and in rich symbols. Yet, not all of the pieces speak to this sense, but sometimes veer towards exclusion, and alienation.

What happens when we don't belong? What happens when this rejection is happening inside our heads? Thomas Mixon's 'Clandestine Depression' touches upon this idea.

Other pieces in the collection toe the line between considerations of belonging, and those of borders. There are the more literal borders, whose arbitrary nature is sometimes highlighted: 'their border lies/invented/as most boundaries' ('hold the line'). Horrifying things happen at these borders, as we see in Karen Kilcup's 'The Uterus Collector'.

What begins to emerge is the collective struggle to find our space, and to inhabit it without fear or danger. Wherever we end up, we live with the knowledge that these borders, and these communities we inhabit, can be both a blessing and a curse.

The collection ends by looking back. Moving through our pieces, and moving through and over borders, boundaries and moments, we must not fail to remember one of the most crucial elements of being human: we live on this planet together.

We wander in history, treading the footsteps of those who inhabited these spaces before us. We are the caretakers now. If we are not careful we risk losing parts of our global community.

We risk seeing so much of our world in past tense only. As our final poem, 'Please Don't Eat the Water' by [jp/p] ends:

> 'but thank you (So Much) for your generous penny
> to The Museum of What Was:
>
> *All contributions*
> *help ushers breathe'*

If we want the spaces that shape and strengthen us to thrive, we need to come together. To understand that we may belong to multiple communities and groups. That borders do not stop us from connecting, from curating, from creating, or from nurturing for those who will come after us and look to these places as somewhere they too can belong.

Foreword

By Maté Jarai

I can still hear the howls of wolves skimming across the molten
glass, the stir of white, peeling up and over our wide-eyed faces,
gaping mouths. I still feel the sweet burn, the radiant sting of one
reality flushing out the toxicity of the other. I can still taste the
wind in my teeth, sense it clinging to my back, as it rips down from
the cliffs. I recall that rush between my feet, the curve, the crash
of cold against my shoulders when I tried too hard, or not hard
enough. When I thought instead of being, when I doubted my
heart, the growls in my gut.

That other me. The one that came before.
Before I feared the pain –
theirs, yours, mine.

I can still feel the love in the depths of my heart, for these friends,
more like me than any other. I still see the words the universe gave
us, as we tore through those wine-dipped clouds. I can still feel the
marks on my cheek, the trails of tears, the cracks at their wake. I
still hear the melodies we wrote, the instrumentals that brought us
all here, to this place –
the unfathomable, the unruled, the chaotic.

I feel tearing. I taste the loneliness. I hear the dark. The trilogy of hurt that sent us charging back here, to all these smiles, to these stony streets, where the sun is a different breed.

We all escaped something to be here, and still, on we run, maybe for just a while.

Because we all have to go back.
'*This is it,*' is always temporary.
'*This is who we are,*' is just a phase.
But what if it doesn't have to be?

How to talk to shy people at parties

By Samantha Carr

First: The shy people didn't go to the party /
unless invited under such circumstances that it
was more perilously painful to say no / or they
had run out of an exhaustive excuse list / from
childcare to watching paint dry.

Second: On running out of excuses, the shy
people brought paint to the party / in order to
distract themselves from the discomfort / of
realising there were more excuses on the other
side of the page.

Third: Put the paint down gently in the kitchen /
and suggest they make themselves a drink / they
won't / instead they will cradle the paint pot
taking small sips when invited to make
Conversation.

Fourth: You then won't remember the shy people
are there / because in many ways they aren't /
your small talk conversations will be glossed with
/ wallflowers of thoughts painted onto the lounge
Walls.

Fifth: Except they'll be so magnolia that it isn't
until later / you notice the fresh flowers they left
behind / and you want to tell them they're
beautiful / and ask why didn't they say
Something.

Sixth: If, on exiting / they look you in the eye and
/ tell you they had a great night / know that
they've spent the evening adding extensively to
that precious excuse list / that the flowers will
fade but you'll always remember them.

Outport

By Hannah Weber

I.

on the nights I can't sleep
I think of the outport:
the rising cliffs,
the tremors of light.
It's good; good like the
brackish sea-fogged wind all down West Street,
good like the chorus of murky white gulls and the hush-hush
of reeds that clothe the trees.

Good like eelgrass, sweetgale, harebells
lulling and sweeping in the blue –
how even silence
        dips out of the landscape.

boundaries and contours emerge and disappear
occur and reoccur

always for the first time

II.

You could forge a heritage in the wilderness, if it came to that.
It's not an act of cowardice, slipping
cupped hands into that river, to drink,
to wash the salt from one's cheeks. Later, retreating to sip on wine
made of nettles, or blueberries.

The present

By Joan García Viltró

Now that we're different animals,
now that we're into this hybrid shape-shifting,
now that we've shed that compliant mindset
       for good,
now that we don't take tomorrow
       for granted,
and live in a short-term eternity
threading our way through shafts of light
       in murky waters,
now that we've dropped out of pointless customs
       like that growing old,
and disown the memory of the slumbering bodies
       we used to inhabit,
and gloat over our bulging, brand new suits,

now that, at last, we're a different species
wandering around dreams we don't feel
       the urge to wake from
          any more,

       now I pledge,
with the slime of having crawled down a birth
       canal again:
this is what I've done to reach out, over
this ever gaping distance, to you.

Charlie's tree

By Devjani Bodepudi

We called it Charlie's Tree, ever since the day little Charlie Evans reappeared beneath it.

One Sunday summer's night, we played by the tree like we always did; Me, Freddie, Charlie and a couple of other kids from the neighbourhood. We hid in the branches and climbed like monkeys; we threw down arrows and spears and hunted our prey, and while we played, we forgot ourselves, just like we always did. But when the yellow streetlights came on, we remembered it was time to go home. We didn't realise at the time, and we only found out late that night when his mother called around to all of our houses, banging on all of our doors in desperation, that Charlie never made it home. He was gone for two whole weeks and no one could say where.

Before all this, we called it the Swinging Tree because there was always a piece of knotted rope tied to one of the boughs for as long as anyone could remember. We would swing on it in turns, back and forth, and then jump off to tumble and roll on the soft mossy floor only a foot or so below.

The tree stood between us and amongst us, right at the centre of our cul-de-sac, on a patch of green that the neighbourhood dogs would sometimes mark as theirs. The council came and mowed the grass occasionally, but we kept the green clean, we met by the tree, and played on it. It was our tree and our green.

We could believe ourselves in a forest, as we lay underneath it; the blue of the sky only just peeking through the gaps between the leaves, which whispered with lost voices of children who grew up and became adults one day. With branches that grew infinitely high, and hung graciously low, it created a world in which we would be recast into something more than what we believed ourselves to be.

In the winter, when it snowed, our tree would remain covered in a decadent frosting for weeks afterwards, and flowers of crystal would bloom on every branch, glistening in the bright winter sun. And when the snow did finally thaw, and we stood underneath, it was our own private rain cloud. It was like magic; soft petals of ice falling all around us, on our noses, on the tops of our heads and running down the backs of our necks, whilst still peeking through the branches, would be blue, blue sky, and not a cloud to be seen.

After the police had come and taken our statements, after the neighbours went around to visit with their food, concern and curiosity, Charlie's mother went to visit the tree.

Wearing an old dressing gown, with her lank, dirty hair falling down and around her face, she leant against the great, wide trunk, slid down to the hard ground, and cried. She wailed so loudly, we could hear her from our house while we ate our dinner of chicken and rice.

"I'll give you anything, I'll do anything, just give me back my little boy," she called up to the branches, up through the spaces between, shrieking and sobbing into the indigo twilight.

Ma shook her head and muttered, "poor woman, I would do exactly the same," and carried on spooning more food onto her plate. I put my spoon down and listened. I had never heard a grown-up cry

18

before. Listening to Charlie's mother fall apart, unsettled me.

We heard Charlie's mother go back every night after that and sometimes we would stand around and watch as she cried. It was like a strange kind of theatre. We watched from a distance, sometimes fighting back nervous giggles when it all became too uncomfortable. It was easier than admitting the guilt we all felt.

Then, exactly nine days later, Charlie reappeared. It was me who found him. A few of us were going to meet at the tree and then cycle to the woods a little farther off. I was the first to arrive and that's when I saw him; at the foot of the tree. He was curled up like a cat, not moving. I dropped my bike and walked slowly over to him. I thought maybe he was dead. I bent down to get a better look, when he opened his eyes. I screamed. He screamed. It would have been funny except it wasn't.

"Where am I?" Charlie sat up and looked around, his eyes darting up and around, before finally resting on me. "How did I get here?"

"Stay there!" I shouted.

I ran to Charlie's house, leaving my bike and Charlie under the tree. I banged on the door until Charlie's mother, Mrs Evans came out. Her mouth drooped in resignation and dark circles had settled like charcoal in the creases under her eyes, but seeing me standing there, she knew. She ran straight to the tree with me, and Charlie was still there.

She held him so tight, I thought he would suffocate but his mother would not let go. She just kept saying, 'thank you' over and over again as she rocked him back and forth. A couple of the other children arrived after that, and before I knew it, everyone on the street had appeared.

We did not go to the woods to play that day. Charlie went home and we sat under the tree and talked about what could have happened. We never did find out because he kept saying he couldn't remember.

That same night, the new couple who had moved in next door a few days before, Beckie and Keith, spent the night under Charlie's tree. They took a tent and their sleeping bags and camped out there until morning. The night was cool and clear, and the evening stars twinkled, growing and shrinking until, one by one, they shrank away to nothing in the ambivalent dawn. Beckie and Keith packed up their tent and went home. When they met Ma, later that day, on their way to the shops, they told her they had decided to try the tree. Maybe it would bring them a baby. They had tried everything else. They were laughing and smiling like mischievous children. They winked like they had done something they shouldn't have, but were extremely proud of, nonetheless, and Ma said, "why not?"

Nothing happened for a few weeks after that, and everything seemed to go back to normal except Charlie's mother would not let her son stay out past five o'clock and she would always be at her door waiting.

Then one morning, Beckie came out of her house carrying a basket of fruit. I was swinging on our front gate, watching her, as I often did. So different to my mother, she wore sundresses that left her arms bare, and the tops of her breasts exposed. Her hair was always loose, and it hung straight and black to where her bra-strap must have been, and that day, her hair shimmered in the sun, pulling into it, all light, trapping it between dark violet strands. I was mesmerised as I watched.

Pulling out the relentless weeds that invaded her garden, tiny beads of sweat formed on Ma's upper lip. She stopped and looked up when she saw Beckie and asked her what she was doing with the basket of fruit. Beckie told her it was because she was expecting, and it was a miracle. She said she knew it sounded stupid, but she thought the tree had something to do with it. She blushed as she spoke, and Ma only nodded. "We are our own gods and our own demons, but it is still important to give thanks, whenever we believe thanks are due." Ma asked Beckie to wait while she went inside. She came out again with a ball of red wool and a pot of vermillion which she had mixed with some mustard oil to make a paste. She walked out to the tree with Beckie, making sure to cover her head with a scarf and then she started to draw a symbol on the rough, silent bark. She made me hold onto one end of the wool and she circled the trunk with the rest of it, unspooling it carefully in infinite crimson loops. Beckie stood with palms together, and head bowed, as instructed by Ma and then placed the basket of fruit under the tree after offering thanks. She smiled at us both and looked up through the branches of Charlie's Tree, her hand shielding her eyes, as if searching for something more.

Freddie's mother, Mrs Wheeler from two doors down, came out to see what we were doing. She could see the tree from her kitchen window, and I wondered what she thought of Ma. She waved and smiled, and Ma waved back, tight-lipped.

"This tree is sacred," Ma said to me and Beckie, and carried on doing whatever she was doing. She stopped and turned to me, then. "No more playing under this tree. Do you understand?"

I nodded. I knew better than to argue with Ma. The next morning the fruit was gone but the basket remained.

That same day, Mr and Mrs Wheeler went to the tree. Arms linked, heads bowed, solemn and thoughtful, they looked like they were talking to it. They left a ten-pound note in the empty basket at the foot of the trunk and walked away quickly, careful not to catch anyone's eye. Like the fruit, the money was gone the next morning.

"What did your parents ask for, Freddie?" we asked him the next day.

"For my dad to find a job. He hasn't worked in ages," replied Freddie. A few days later, Freddie came running to us with news. His dad had found a job with the railways. It was perfect, he said.

After that, people went to the tree and left all sorts of gifts. The gifts were always gone by the next morning and no one seemed to question it, not until things started to go wrong.

Charlie's dad was caught having an affair and he left. Charlie stopped playing out for a while and Charlie's mother was seen every morning leaving empty bottles in her recycling bin, the clank-clunk as the bottles fell against each other echoing through the Close.

Beckie bloomed. She was out more, sunbathing in the back garden and she was always smiling as she placed her hands in front of her belly, unthinkingly framing the tiny life growing inside her. But then they found out Keith only had months to live. The doctors had found a tumour which spread through his whole body. Any treatment could prolong his life only a little, they said, and he would be in too much pain through it all. It was too late. The doctors agreed it would take a miracle, but hadn't they already had their miracle?

22

Beckie asked.

A few days after Mr Wheeler started his new job, Freddie's mum had a stroke. She was so young, the same age as Ma. Everyone from our street went to see her in hospital and always came back saying it was such a shame. When Mrs Wheeler was finally released, she had lost the use of the left side of her body, leaving her with only half a grimace, for a smile, if she smiled.

People started saying that the tree was cursed. Everyone who had asked for something, ended up losing something, they said.

Ma offered to do a special ceremony that would help. She said it was just bad luck and jealous spirits. She said, sometimes people were envious when they saw other people happy and that's when bad things happen. The tree had nothing to do with it, she said, it was only there to channel the good, the good that people themselves had the power to bring about. But no one trusted her superstitious mumbo-jumbo, as they called it and whispered that perhaps she was always a bit strange.

"Mandy, no offence or anything," Mr Wheeler said to her one day, "but we don't need that here, not in this day and age. Maybe, where you're from, all this is normal, but I thought you were different. You live here, now."

"Her name's Mandira," I told Mr Wheeler, looking him straight in the eye, as if this was his only mistake. Ma said nothing and went back into our house. She came out with more holy paraphernalia and her head covered in defiance. I watched on, helpless and embarrassed. She walked around two houses; ours and Beckie's, because they were joined. Waving an incense stick and muttering words in a language I did not recognise, she scattered red chillies on the ground, making a large ring of metaphorical fire for protection, she explained. Finally, she hung half a garland of green chillies and lime from the door frame. Jealous spirits did not like hot and sour, I guessed.

In the meantime, the rest of the street were mourning. Everyone blamed the tree and some people blamed Ma as well. No-one was allowed to play near the tree again and Charlie and Freddie didn't come out to play with me at all.

The yarn Ma had tied around the great trunk was still there but now it clung grubby and loose. The rope swing which had hung so resolutely all these years, lay tattered and frayed upon the floor like a broken noose, and people stayed away from the tree.

Before the summer was done, when the pavement was still too hot to walk on with bare feet, the leaves on Charlie's Tree began to turn. Yellow, to orange, to red until they fell finally, to a form a dry and restless carpet.

"It sleeps," Ma said, "because all its love is spent, and no one cares for it anymore."

September came and it was time to go back to school. The small patch of grass where the tree stood, lay neglected and barren, dank and patchy. It looked like winter when we looked outside our windows.

Keith became sicker but Mrs Wheeler started to recover. Charlie's dad never came back and all the bad luck either disappeared or got worse and everyone still blamed the tree.

One night, when the Harvest moon hung heavy and low, I stood at my bedroom window watching the night sky. I saw Beckie leave her house and forget to close the door behind her.

Carrying a large candle, her face was illuminated by its sallow light. She walked slowly and looked straight ahead until she reached the tree. Her head was not bowed now, and she did not smile. She no longer wore sundresses and her hair was tied. The branches stood bare; silvered in the moonlight like the white hairs of an old dog and Charlie's Tree looked as if it had given up.

Placing the candle on the ground, Beckie picked up a large fallen branch. She touched it to the flicker of light on the floor, and the branch flared to life with bright orange ribbons of flame, dripping and leaping precariously from where Beckie held it.
Trapped in a tight snarl, Beckie's face was transformed. Her eyes were alight with the fire they reflected, her mouth drooled with a hunger for vengeance, and she at once, became a demoness like in the stories Ma used to tell.
The tree bowed as low as it could go, but it was old now, and too stiff to bend far. Head pulled back, Beckie's gaze reached the top of the mighty oak. She thrust her flames into the tree, again and again and again. It took a moment before anything happened and then all at once, the tree was alive with light, contorted in pain where it stood. One by one, they came out of their homes; Charlie's mother and the Wheelers among them. All of their eyes were lit up with fire and hate. Now, they all looked like demons, holding their own boughs of flames.

All night, the tree twisted and turned, the flames leaping and cart-wheeling in a kind of tethered freedom as it stood rooted, burning alive.

The adults watched, growling and glowering, but at peace when the moon finally set, when the flames finally died and all that was left was the charred shell of the mighty tree that once was ours. One by one, they all went back to their homes as I watched from my bedroom window. I scarcely knew what I had seen. Exhausted, I fell to my floor until my mother came in to find me hours later and I told her what had happened.

"But it stands as it always has," she said.

When I looked out of the window, I saw she was right. "But how could she be?" I thought. When I examined it later that day, I could see patches of blackened earth on the green, and I believed I could smell the almost imperceptible scent of burning, but the tree still stood, just as it always had.

The funeral was in October. Keith willed himself to get better, stronger, for a time, but he didn't last long. He died peacefully, Beckie said. She moved away before Christmas, and we never saw her again and no-one mentioned the demons in the night.

Sometimes, I go back to visit my mother. The neighbourhood has changed; all our old neighbours have moved away. The grassy bank remains as does Charlie's Tree but now it is just a tree. No-one talks of it because there is no one left to remember. But there is an almost imperceptible smell of burning, sometimes, when the breeze is blowing in the right direction. And at times, my mother will look out of her kitchen window, and I will follow her gaze to where the tree still stands.

And sometimes there is the sound of a rustle through leaves, which whisper with lost voices of children who grew up and became adults one day.

DREAMBATH

By Chloe Elliott

Somewhere a storm
is coming. I am in a pool
that is green without fish.
This is mean of my mind but
I am at least awarded Sophie.
We cling together on a flamingo
pool-float. She asks me to get a picture
but my fingers are wet so the phone won't
capture it. Then she finds her
family and has dinner but I can't find mine.
I dig out the water. There
are a series of lagoons.
I enter a pool I am not
allowed in. It is green and
almost has fish. My mind is
mean like that. I press my
foot against the filter and
make clam chowder. All
the buckets nod as I strain
the stock. The grit piles at the drain.
I go back to the normal pool.
I get sucked in by a pit.
The pit curls round like a zero
gravity simulator. I think it is
worth trying to find my parents
from underneath so I dip under

but it is too tightly packed,
there are too many white people.
When I look under the surface
they don't have feet but instead
that which resembles crabsticks
or dynamite or birthday candles.
Let me resolve this. I miss you.
Everyday. Everyone too white to be mine,
pronouncing congee as clam chowder.
I put up MISSING posters on all the lamps
in the park. Poolside buffet. The filter stopped
working a week ago so the whole compound
is underwater.
I'm dishing this up as a reward. The winner will
pretend to drink out of a purple sandcastle.
I'm best friends with a komodo dragon. I'm closing
my eyes so I can't see where it goes.

Brighella

the songwriter

By Jake Reynolds

It's time to return to Georgia so that everything makes sense,
my body cast by headlights shining in a circle around me.
It makes me feel like the last standing protestor, or the bad side
of sunset over a strip of seats on a slow-moving train.
I don't cry in my song because the song is sad, but because I think
of us feeling ashamed to hear it.
Still, this dirge, weather forecast ordained, isn't about you.
The student smokers congregated by the main entrance
instead of the heaving garden aren't about you,
and nor are the waiting taxis or the chefs dumping large
sacks into the bins. I'd be damned to throw this praise back at you,
worse still to let it calcify inside me and build on a brittle crust.

How borders were drawn in straight lines

By Antony Owen

"We will never let our hold to this land go,
to let it go it will be like throwing away our mother that gave us birth"
Aitooweyah – Principal Chief of the Cherokee

This savage millinery shall pass –
when blunt blades moan across worn leather
a strange headdress is taken and an immigrant boy accepts his fate.

Last night, that boy ate rancid chicken singing slave songs to a
chain of stars
and all-American boys smoked tales of long dead trees
blowing into his face so he would dream Cherokee.

This broken horse shall pass mists
rising in the distance from whistling mouths and earholes.
It is August in Dakota and all the wolves are studying men who
leave morsels.

These savage wagons leave wigwams of skin
rain comes down like thorny arrows from the yew.
A Sioux boy blows smoke at his sister trying to wake the dead.
rapids.

Last night she combed her hair with whale bone and felt the blood
of her scalp drip cold upon her palms as she patted her soul on
palominos.
The road is glowing with soldiers who used to trade.

This gentle child has passed —
she untied the horses and watched them run like rapids.
A hawk emerged from the mist, making his peace with
forefathers in the wind.

In between

By Colette Tennant

I've always lived in between
Aunt Myra who insisted I use military-strict manners –
spoons and forks parallel, polished and exact as a Roman phalanx,
and my grandmother who refused to wear a bra,
who, on our way home from the store, sat me on a park bench next
to her
so we could eat butterscotch straight out of the jar.
And when I went to family reunions, I didn't resemble anybody
really,
but when a distant relative said I looked just like my dad,
I wanted it to be true.
The women I golfed with didn't know about my Ph.D.
and my creative writing students wouldn't guess I've been accused
of hitting a tennis ball as hard as a man.
When I visited my Appalachian cousins,
they told me I talked funny,
and when I moved to Virginia, they called me a damn Yankee.
I was somewhere between terror and nervous laughter
when my son-in-law said he'd gone to an estate sale
and bought a bike frame, a gun, and one frozen duck.

Anyone adopted feels pretty much in between.
I imagine most people do if they admit it, all of us
like the middle scoop in a banana split, flavors all blurred,
a traffic light stuck on caution,

a thin piece of cheese in a sandwich made with thick bread,
a faucet that can't decide between hot and cold,
like that hour in the morning when you've finished your coffee,
but you still aren't completely awake
on this planet spinning between all those fickle stars
and that wily smile of the moon.

Clandestine depression

By Thomas Mixon

There's a sadness under all my other sadnesses,
which I've plenty of, but there's one I keep
obscured, confined to reap the mere rewards
of irreverent depths. A grief only defined
by where it is, and its lack of access
to anything outside of it, and my belief
that it was there for years before I knew it.
Sometimes I swim toward it, and it toward me,
neither willing to breaststroke beyond
a buoyed border of enormous breadth,
buoys no birds land upon. They bob
up and down for hours after both of us
stop moving. On the surface I am gracious,
offer up a fish market's supply of sadness,
the smell so strong it covers up the hidden one,
abyssal, redolent of numbers less than zero,
dewy with a clinging mud, content to sink
as deep as wishes go when you pretend to throw
a penny in a fountain, impossible to find
later, when you're home, a savage hole
instead of pockets, stained with current,
apropos of riptide, shallowing of soul.

Patch of Blue

By Phillip Crymble

Jerry Goldsmith's title theme, its plaintive
minor key arrangement, somehow welcoming
the snow that falls outside our kitchen window.
The rote activity of washing takes me
miles away, and in that sweetest dream
the music like a hand-embroidered
counterpane — each note within the melody
a cipher to be read and kept concealed.
That we communicate at all is half
mistake. I turn the thick LP, listen
to the piano, all the silences it leaves —
the hiss and crackle whispering of things
so old they beggar history: a sound
like fire in fields of wheat — the wind at sea.

How to heal a broken heart

By Joe Lucking

In the Spring, through places once Verboten, we wander freely in a
much-changed Berlin.

The discovery of an old passport resuscitates recollections of a cold
war visit and I am borne
ceaselessly into the past.

Then it is winter.

At the Helmstedt-Marienborn border crossing, a fresh-faced
young man takes a seat on the
West Berlin bound train. As their colleagues photograph from the
platform, armed
Grenztruppen board and sit opposite. Like psychiatrists, they wait
for him to speak.

The train passes through Magdeburg, Brandenburg, and Potsdam.

They watch him watching a whirring grey landscape of strip lights
and Trabants.

A studious young woman reading Schopenhauer asks, *"Wie lange
wird es dauern, bis das
Ende der Welt erreicht ist?"*

"How long will it take to reach the end of the world?"

She repeats the question, the young man transfixed by her beauty is unable to answer.

An invisible force forbids him to take her hand as they stroll along Friedrichstrasse toward
the DDR fortifications. Despite or perhaps because of it, she beckons him to follow her into a
sparse black and white Alexanderplatz where they sit next to the Fountain of International
Friendship. She asks for a cigarette and magically produces a technicolour copy of Die Rote
Fahne from under her duffle coat.

In this monochrome scene, only her lips are full and red as though all blood has been drained from her body.

"Je langsamer das Leben wird, desto schneller nähert sich der Moment."

"The slower life becomes, the more quickly the moment approaches."

They float to Flora Straße, then Wollank Straße, cordoned-off areas, dangerous places full of
ever-vigilant soldiers, dead ends, bombed-out empty spaces, and acne-faced buildings pockmarked by bullets. On to Mitte, Friedrichshain, then Lichtenberg, Prenzlauer and Pankow they roam.

42

Until they reach the grand socialist avenue Leipziger Straße, straining to connect with Potsdamer Platz, the wall in all its momentous greyness preventing it from
doing so.

At one of those Berlin tenements with courtyard after courtyard, where everything ends and
dissolves into silence, she vanishes.

Those we have loved are now strangers, calcified into irrelevance by absence, the great
falsifier.

Later, the love-struck baby-faced tourist came across a memorial to those who lost their lives
attempting to cross.

It was as if not only time had stopped under the weight of the dead, but the very perception of it had been obliterated.

The dead in cold possession of the centuries, ephemeral figures with an evasive remoteness
about them, beset by the shadows of silent and hidden catastrophes the details of which
follow them to the grave. Those odd people, skulking in the wings, their desperation, grief,
and hope racing into a past that constitutes us.

Hold the line

By LM Cole

the margin snails   the margin shells
edged   serrated   not a knife
they have not   split flesh   spilt blood
and so have not been named toothed
I have found   in them   an embrace
softer   still   than sun-soaked silt soil
underfoot   and yet have   not
understood where   their border lies
invented   as most boundaries
wavering   as the line of the sea

Grandfather's rubble wall

By Melissa Burrage

Elves did not build our rubble wall. Grandfather and his grandfather before him built our wall in the **farmer's** precinct of a Boston suburb, when this land served as a border between one farm **and another, kept** the ox, cow and chickens from escaping. Stonework three and four feet high **zig zag across our** land. Common rubble walls like this snake throughout New England hills **and woodlands.** Men and women foraged for stone then, found much of it in the **soil** when ploughing: igneous and metamorphic rock of irregular shapes and sizes, **granite made round** by glaciers and erosion, slabs split from ledge using chisel, wedge and **hammer. These amateur** stoneworkers hauled random rocks into piles, packed the soil down with **shovel, hoe and foot,** rolled the heavy boulders into place, making their legs and a wooden plank do much of the work, leveling with string and brash, laying patiently without mortar—a dry wall—which seldom cracks or shifts when frost appears, impervious to nature's forces. They filled the top of their wall with random smaller stones and pebbles, left gaps and gateways with rails and posts for neighbors **to pass through.** My ancestors used this wall to throw their trash behind before there was a town dump, where one can still find broken chamber pot lids once tucked beneath **Victorian beds, medicinal bottles,** cure-all serums used to heal wounds, like Lydia Pinkham's **Vegetable Compound for Female Weakness,** Dr. Kilmer's Swamp Root, or Uncle Arthur's whiskey jug, swigs likely taken in secret behind the barn. When I moved to the ancestral home in the '80s, the stone wall needed repair. A house had just been built on the neighboring land where the wildflowers once grew. Workers blasted granite ledge with dynamite, trucks rumbled and **shook the** land, cement mixers poured a foundation and swimming pool. Grandfathers' **stone wall spilled** down in the chaos. It bothered me to see the broken wall, for I remembered it as **a child and** didn't like the mess. I could not let my ancestors' **hard work,** years of patient tending, cascade down, collapse. I hauled the tumbled rocks **back into place,** lifting, rolling, setting, bursting my appendix in the process, feeling warm **fluid escape the thin** pouch within my belly. It's not so much that I want to keep anyone out, **for you are welcome here,** but I choose to honor and remember those who came before me on this sacred ancestral ground. I repair to keep the earlier generations alive. There is no signature on this work of art that surrounds my yard, and yet I hear family stoneworkers speaking. I feel strength from a wall that still stands long after those who built it are gone. I know who built our wall. It wasn't the elves.

Note—Poem written in response to Robert Frost's "Mending Wall"

Folk tale from the old country

By Vanessa Ackerman

Inside the great night
long ago
the silver cry of a child
The mother, dead
carved up like an arctic whale
Laughter when all awoke
(tell the story
the more you look at it, the greener it becomes)
Alive again , the mother banged on her drum
come to dinner
laughed as she gazed into your mirror
wept as she plunged
her dry death fingers
here are my jewels
no mine
not even stone you whispered
the moral is
this image is yours
hold it like you might
a young bird
sit at the table
the bird on your lap
while you talk while you eat

stroke its slimy feathers
it has found you
feed the unfed bird

These lines drawn in the sand which you call borders

By Lianne O'Hara

a bird in flight flaps / once / twice / thrice / echoes resonate weakly
/ in foreign skies / it dips /

too

sudden / falls / wets its beak / tumbles / traces a journey in reverse
/ before / wet wings

regenerate /

oral histories / before / muffled sound became regular speech /
before / the rocking of the sea /

ceased to be a cradle / and became a coffin / before / debts were
settled without warning /

before / in

cold rooms entire lives were repeated / before / policemen ground-
ed in disbelief / before / a

memory

became a lie / before / trauma became truth / sought after / before
/ a stamp is pressed onto

paper /

wings presented as fortune / as stability / as a welcome / change
from home / left behind for

no

reason / only to slip through / the nets / hoisted by borders / called
us / and them / because

before / the only travel north was a return / with riches /

and gifts / the exotic fruits of pillage /
and
plunder / renders anyone travelling / empty-handed / a suspect /
before / a declaration is made
/
upon arrival old wings / are clipped / feathers of home plucked to
facilitate / assimilation / or
erasure of culture / of love / of kindness / of what sparked flight to
begin with / before / burning
wings there should be water / not wax / knot nets to break falls /
not to capture / birds in flight /
flap / once / twice / thrice / hoping / for an echo / of new life /

Cloud seeding in Beijing

By JB Jørgensen

On the day of the jubilee Beijing hides behind a white haze
which makes my eyes burn, steals focus and definition
like the VPN which cycles endlessly, a hamster in its wheel.
In the park ladies weave satin ribbons in the air,
teach me to form bright characters which disappear
before anyone can decipher them
and a man dips a long-handled brush in the lake
traces calligraphy on the flagstones.
Words evaporate as sun warms the ground
merges with the humid air, our breath and whispers
perhaps falling as rain tomorrow, clearing the air
as what we cannot say draws tear tracks on window panes.

The time I saw my father cry
By Mary Mulholland

My eyes are deep set like yours, but green
and sclera-scarred from when you made
me look at the sun in water.

When my eye pressures rise I see stars.
You taught me the night sky, to not-fear the dark,
do what others just talk about, ignore taunts.

You weren't so tough. I found what you wrote
all those years I pretended you didn't exist,
the guilt now mine. And how

you clung to life, no longer aware,
watchful eyes beneath your knotted glare
Or you'd play the piano, a dance starting

in your mind, When they begin the beguine.
Again. Again. Resisting the final refrain.
If I asked if you were afraid, you frown.

That last morning even your eyes listened
as I listed your loved ones on the other side.
I opened a window, heard a sigh and turned.

You'd stopped breathing.
Your eyes were pooling with tears –

Where is home for you?
By Maria Cohut

When he asks this question, at first I don't know what to say. Home is Bucharest, city of dust, where dreams travel on the subway, no ticket, hand in hand with rowdy teenagers who have just landed a 10 in Latin class despite the fact that they've barely attended all year, and by way of prayer they go bar-hopping between Amzei and Universtății, censing every corner with the heady tobacco of their cigarettes. Home is Coventry, city of ruins and thankless industry, sown with fusion all-you-can-eats and cheap watering holes where you can go drown and no one will ask any questions, long shadow of Godiva's self-righteous nudity, stretched thin between FarGo and Canley, so thin that you can poke its ribs through the crumbling asphalt.

And who is this guy, anyway, what claim does he have to the history of my belonging?

Bucharest, despite everything, raised me to be polite, but Coventry taught me how to stand my ground, so I answer question with question. What does he mean by that?

He means, he clarifies with insufficient embarrassment, where I come from. As I open my mouth to form the sounds of origin, of the place I didn't choose, but had to grow in and mould my body to, I want to try and explain. I want to tell him about Coventry market, where they sell bowls of fruit and veggies for one quid, where I buy pickled vine leaves and trays of baklava from the Algerian stall, where a seller of metal T-shirts once hailed my mom with 'how can I help you, mami?' and she giggled, and picked shirts with loud wolf and moon prints for each of my cousins. I want to tell him about my neighbour who wears her gauzy, colourful veil tight like skin-soldered armour and never utters a word, though she always smiles the brightest smile when she sees me, and about my other neighbour, who never lifts her eyes from her old Nokia to look at me when I say 'hi', always texting someone as though the future of the world depended on the uninterrupted motion of her fingers on the keys. Then I want to tell him about my old high-school, two hundred years old and counting, looking every bit its age, holding its weight on tiptoes with the grace and hesitation of uneasy privilege, of the sanctity of the teachers' fumoir, and the off-limits backyard that I and my friends could sneak into if we made sweet eyes to doamna Doina, the administrator. I want to convey the mundane thrill of the 116 bus, with its stations of the urban cross - Orăşelul Copiilor, Bellu Cemetery, Tineretului, and so on until Unirii - that little theatre on wheels that taught me all the faces of human drama in under four years.

When the words 'I'm from Romania' find their way out, I will them to carry the lights, sounds, smells of all my homes. Yet he seems to hear even less than what I offer.

He went to Romania once, years ago. He was in Bucharest for a couple of days, and of course that gives him the authority to tell me what he thinks I should know about this home of mine, this place that birthed me, what he believes I ought to be embarrassed about by default. Seldom has he seen so much poverty, he says, and oh, the corruption. I wonder what ever he could know about either poverty or corruption, this man with a flashy Rolex on his wrist and shiny patent leather shoes at a work conference in a five-star hotel. I would like to ask him, but his speech has grown ever more animated, and now he demands to know how come I was able to make it as far as my second home. Did my parents work for the Party? He knew somebody once who was able to get away because his parents had been loyal to the Party - maybe not in Romania, maybe this guy he once knew was from Bulgaria or Hungary, he forgets, but it doesn't matter anyway, it's all the same, isn't it. This is not a question, so I say nothing.

Nothing is required of me except my obedient attention, so I shift it towards the warm orange light of the free-for-all bar. The man, who introduced himself to me earlier, but whose name I refuse to remember, notices this and offers to retrieve a drink for me. I'll do it myself, I say, I'm an old woman and my joints are all stiff, I need to move a little. I see it then, a flicker of disappointment – or is it disgust - in his Dior-bespectacled eyes, and he turns away without a word, naturally falling into conversation with a taller, slimmer young woman in the next group.

At the bar, a tightly uniformed bartender offers me their services in a recognisable Eastern European lilt. I know I shouldn't, but an echo chamber locked up deep within me begs to be unbolted. In that moment, I yearn for recognition, for a glimmer of borrowed camaraderie. I ask the bartender where they are from and I hastily add, before their smile gets a chance to stiffen in an act of practised depersonalization, that I'm from Romania. That's my excuse, and I offer it with the greed of a starving guest. I pray this is enough, but when they answer 'Slovenia' and slap my tumbler of Laphroaig on the counter I can tell the conversation is dead and I'm guilty of its murder.

I go on to sip my Laphroaig on my own, in silence, at a corner table, while scrolling conspicuously through social media - the 'please don't talk to me' strategy of women everywhere. My friend Pei has gone on a trip to Bali and is sharing photos of resorts as perfect as stage sets. Corina is delighted to announce that she has secured another research scholarship, this time somewhere in the States. Paul has taken the leap and self-published his novel, about a French guy studying abroad in Spain, after many years of rejections from agents. His sentences, one agent generously told him in the rejection email, are too long-winded, difficult to follow, hard to sell to an anglophone readership. Had he tried to pitch to a continental indie press yet? What about Virginia Woolf's chewy phrases, Paul had replied at the time to resounding silence.

From two tables over, I hear sonorous, forced, baritone laughter. It belongs to the man from before, who has cornered another woman. She is young, petite, wears a fashionable kimono-cut tunic whose loose right sleeve the man keeps touching compulsively as the rest of the garment shrinks ever deeper into the plush seat on its wearer's cue.

Where is home for you, I overhear him asking. I don't catch her answer, she must be very quiet, but he follows up with an anecdote about Taipei.

Orgullosa gringa peruana
By Liana Kalpeke-Dale

Cuando *escribo mi poesía en español*,
do I appropriate the language?

My skin identifies me as *una gringa*,
but my heart feels mixed-race:

at least half Peruvian and maybe more,
brown-skinned brown-eyed

eating scarce vegetarian *Chifa* with friends
mixing and matching funny insults *con la boca llena*,

carajo and *mierda* and *pendejo*
then throw in a *conchatumare*, of course.

When I tattoo Peru behind my left ear
where above bone there is only skin

do I appropriate its borders?
Where is the line between

to appropriate and
to honor?

When my lover back in Lima

when he'd kiss me as though kissing were
a wholly new act, as though

no word existed for what he did
con su lengua,

when he'd kiss me, thirsty,
then touch me and say every time

with pupils dilated,
Estás mojadita,
        when we made love –
        not when we had sex, not when we fucked

        and I knew I never had before
        (and know now I haven't since) –
        did I appropriate his love?

When I finally left Peru,

white face blotchy from crying
mixed-race heart heavy, heavy

with tears the size of *monedas*
that fell, collecting in my shoes

like the rainwater *que nunca caye* in Lima,
did I cede whatever right I'd earned

to think of it as *mi hogar*

adoptado? And if I return, ten years later,

can I reclaim that right
or can I only appropriate it?

Mientras tanto, my green dreams prefer
Barranco, Miraflores, San Isidro

and the deep, briny blue living so close
to *la costa verde*, so very very *verde*,

that you'd mistake them for two
lovers sleeping together in their bed.

Dreams cannot appropriate
land *ni* culture *ni* art

but long before I slept,
Peru appropriated my dreams.

Now I dream in Spanish,
America's own *orgullosa gringa peruana*:
proud Peruvian gringa.

Undocumented

By Tricia Gates Brown

Coiled around me, helix of sleep
and dream, erasing space not you or me.
Not for fear, more reaching

for a handrail, as you held
my arm in new company, talked fast,
tap dance of manners—top hat and vanilla smile.

Okay, maybe fear. Tricks to stump
suspicion: Yes, Sir. Beautiful day, Sir.
Can I help with that, Sir?—getting on the good

side of white. I watched you serve, work, weigh
reactions to swarthy eyes and accent,
signing Father, Son, Holy Ghost like cops

stacked the deck to find you.
Will they know you broke laws to have
work matter, wanting just a house

like your dad, a bath, shed of tools, tidy
kitchen with chilies and lime? One safe thing
this side of motherland?

Brown dad taught what he could

By Christian Lozada

Because Brown Dad preferred to work in silence,
the instructions were all but nonexistent,
even the directions sit, watch, and learn
were understood for fear of flaring nostrils
and bugged out Filipino eyes that seemed to go
all black like a shark's before it decides to bite.
Watch him cleaver the meat, smashing, breaking,
separating bones and flesh with the same blade
he uses to prune trees outside, see him chop off
the ends of an onion and peel its skin through the tears,
add inaccurate amounts of store-bought sauces
from jars scrolling Asian characters bought
from the Vietnamese market but you're sure
is Korean. Don't you dare ask, though,
because learning happens during the act
and speaking happens when the job is one.

Brown Dad taught what he could, but failed
to teach us anything beyond what he knew:
do this to chicken because you will live alone,
maybe away from family or what you find safe
and save money because your name only counts on paper
and pay for your children's college because Lolo paid mine
and carry what you owe.

Brown Dad taught what he could and little more.
His knowledge began and ended with debt, property, isolation,
but his gaps in the competition with classmates and coworkers
is where love lies, and I never share what I owe.

Let me be your Ruth

By Sabrina Sanchez

from the moment I saw you,
a sojourner, I found my home
that which I'd follow out of Moab

I tried to stay away in truth but
then you pursued, capricious
still, there with me nonetheless

and that was all I could ever ask,
that you cling to me as I do you,
let me make my sacrifices

I wanted your God and people
to be my God and people,
and I tried so dearly to believe

my arduous labors would never
fill your coffers, and I couldn't
buckle at another's feet

bought and sold like your affections,
this land we'd shared soon tore
with I, a small piece of the diaspora

Shikii (Tracks)

By Tamiko Mackison

I stood in the doorway
You had removed your slippers
Left them in the corridor

You were gliding Across the tatami floor
Towards the dining table
Where I once laid out hojicha tea

You warmed your feet
On the kotatsu under The blanket
Closed your eyes

You couldn't see me

I was sliding back and forth
Fusing with the paper fusuma doors
Immovable horizontal Tracks

Unable to move forwards towards you
Join you at the table
Couldn't travel back to the front door
Leading to the world I left behind

I stood in the doorway

Air it out
By Bekah Steimel

Nature, They/Them
violated, starved, fed the fuck up,
drew back, swirled a genius pathogen potion, ripped a roar louder
than a jungle rave across all airwaves, Category six flex, and we all
breathed a little faster, if we kept breathing
Their revenge huffed, and it puffed, and blew souls away, reunited
estranged Pangea,
    piece
  by newly shaped piece,
even whispered and winded it's way past the cold shoulder of
Antarctica
But the oceans,
  The oceans
    laid low,
      and waved
          and waved
            and waved
Sea turtles, painfully squirming out of time in their hourglass
figures, sea turtles, already slipped away, sea turtles, upside down
on a coffee table
  Fish swimming in dwindling schools that are not virtual, fish that
have all the oxygen their gills can filter, flipping us a fin, or fish that
float
because they choked on something we swallowed
devoid of Apex dignity, Sharks that pool on a spoon, Sharks in a

The oceans and seas have the upper hand at the lower level
We should hang our heads and apologize through masks, coughs,
short breaths, long pauses, panting, grunting, wheezing, until the
tubing obstructs our remorse
Any regret expressed maskless is yet another unveiled atrocity, is
another reason next time
next time, the oceans
  The oceans
    will lay low,
      and wave
        and wave
          and wave
            and laugh with all the oxygen
              such a deserved ridiculing will require.

The uterus collector

By Karen Kilcup

ICE's mission is to protect America from cross-border crime and illegal immigration that threaten national security and public safety.
--U.S. Immigration and Customs Enforcement

That's what the women name
the man called a doctor
who works for ICE
in a private Georgia prison,
who believes that brown
women who want
asylum are irregular
and need treatment:
their wombs removed
without their knowledge
or consent. He speaks
a different language,
brings no translator,
gathers specimens,
collects federal cash.
Those who threaten
to expose him are
silently sent back
to places they had quit
in hope and fear:
Nigeria, Guatemala, Mexico.

The nurse who blows the whistle
is Black. Her name is Dawn.

For the patients who endure,
hysterectomy is a disembodied
word composed of ancient parts.
It means nothing. It has no past.
It promises no future.

Home: An ode to my ancestors

By Aybike Ahmedi

From the secrets of the Silk Road to Anatolia
A bridge built
Of migrants as they search for home.

Twisted tongues in foreign languages
Created homes
In desolate villages

They brought life and new hope,
But always try to cope
With a past unknown.

The bridge extended
Across the Atlantic
New roots once more planted,

But hands still firmly bound,
Now, not one, but two
Lineages left behind.

Fears of assimilation,
Adverse symptoms, perils of migration.
A new generation

Born with vivid dreams of worlds that come together,
Endeavors to sew seams between cultures and bind traditions
The hand that threads ties between you and me

I dance amongst my hearts' desires
And the boundaries set
By ancestors never met

I toil in agony
In search of Central Asia—
Her hidden histories

My genealogy branched out
In webs of trauma
Passed on to haunt

You, then me.
But understand,
In the end,

We'll all return home
To the same soil and dirt
As we are laid into the earth.

Misunderstood marshal

By Keko Prijatelj

You jailed
Tribes to free
People to live
Where the poor can be fat
And a beggar blonde

You had a dog
The german shepherd turned into poodles
And brought a
Capitalism of stories
Characters, tongues

As a boy you grew
Into a man grew out
Of your village your city
Your country, people had to migrate
You to a foreign land
Far enough and now

Everyone can see you as you truly are

Please don't eat the water
By [jp/p]

Nevermind the fish,
    swimming backwards & upside-down
      overhead; over here, from here
they seem fine

  The trees aren't talking,
    let's say: per se.
  They're laughing; it's their last
  good goddamn laugh

  And no, the birds aren't breathing,
  (Who could ever tell?)   But anyway,
        they still wake us up
          at every ass-hour early

Little ugly vegetables which, let's be hon-
est: none of us ever cared for, they'
 re   not exactly migratory now,   but
  sure, why not   &&

disregard the hardware stores: filled to the gills
with walls & miles of legless headless Tasty! Meat!
this is their service — to us, the surplus, to the gift
      of teeth,   with a need to tear

The ocean,   our sour ocean (of thee I sing) albeit
    she's a few shades shy, of plum   — say
violet, lilac, boysenberry?   — they say
it's just plastic + a couple hyperactive   core reactors

    Just avoid, if you can, looking quite directly
  at any or all   of the spiders   snakes   possums
mice or ants   They burn. And they're just
    not that fond of us anymore

but thank you (So Much) for your generous penny
    to The Museum of What Was:

      All contributions
      help ushers breathe

Acknowledgements

The biggest thank you to all our contributors. To each of those present in this collection, for embraacing this theme so close to our hearts. And to the many voices from all around the world that we have had the pleasure of working with and featuring, both in print and on our website, since our launch in 2018.

To the amazing Cephalopress team, past and present, who work tirelessly whenever they can, in between jobs, late at night, keeping our little press alive, and helping to give a voice to the voiceless.

And finally, to all our readers. We are able to exist because of your support. And we hope to bring you many more Cephalopress titles in the years to come.

Maté Jarai
Editor-in-Chief

Printed in Great Britain
by Amazon

16883074R00058